the

BAPTISM

with the

HOLY SPIRIT

R. A. TORREY

BETHANY HOUSE PUBLISHERS
Minneapolis, Minnesota

"Wait for the Promise of the Father" (Acts 1:4).

"Ye shall be baptized with the Holy Ghost not many days hence" (Acts 1:5).

"Ye shall receive power, after that the Holy Ghost is come upon you" (Acts 1:8).

"For to you is the promise, and to your children, and to all that are afar off, even as many as the Lord our God shall call unto him" (Acts 2:30, ASV).

The Baptism With the Holy Spirit
R. A. Torrey

ISBN 0-7642-0019-4

Copyright © 1972

Cover design by Melinda Schumacher

Published by Bethany House Publishers
11400 Hampshire Avenue South
Bloomington, Minnesota 55438

Bethany House Publishers is a division of
Baker Publishing Group, Grand Rapids, Michigan.

Printed in the United States of America

Foreword

The Apostle Paul said to Timothy, his son in the faith, "The things that thou hast heard from me among many witnesses, the same commit thou to faithful men who shall be able to teach others also." In this short verse we have an interesting chain of witness. *Paul* committed the things he knew concerning God and His salvation to Timothy. Timothy was to commit these things to *faithful men* and these faithful men were to teach *others* also.

Like the Apostle Paul, R. A. Torrey wanted to commit the things that he had learned as a disciple of Jesus Christ to others. He published several "How To" books, *How to work for Christ, How to study the Bible*, etc. He passed on a record of his experiences to other ministers who would follow after him.

From the standpoint of sequence, R. A. Torrey and D. L. Moody were the links between the great Charles Finney revivals in the mid 1800's and the present evangelical and charismatic movement.

Torrey was 19 years old when Finney died in 1875. He was 43 years old when Moody died in 1899, and he was teaching the baptism with the Holy Spirit during the time when Pentecostalism began to rise at the turn of the century. Incidentally, Billy Sunday was 66 and Billy Graham was 10 when Torrey died in 1928. These dates do not explain or include the many ways and voices God used to work His work in the last few generations, *but* they do show us that the witness concerning the Spirit-filled life has not been silent.

Many God-sent leaders such as Finney, Moody and the circuit riders, who preached throughout our country as it moved to the West, had a message that pressed the points of responsibility towards God: repentance and faith in Jesus Christ, and the power of the blood to purify the heart. They taught that Christ also could give power to witness by the filling or the baptism with the Holy Spirit. This was the message that Torrey preached. No doubt these men, together with Torrey, have influenced the Pentecostal and charismatic movement of our day.

Foreword

Another evidence that shows the way in which Torrey sought to commit the ministry to faithful men is shown in his relationship to the Bible school movement in America. Torrey's outreach is also shown in his world-wide ministry in China, Japan, Australia, New Zealand, India, Germany, and the United Kingdom. Pastors, students, and thousands of common people who attended his meetings entered into new power and grace.

This Dimension edition of the *Baptism with the Holy Spirit* shows the clear scriptural teaching that Torrey presented to his audiences. He taught that men should have their faith rooted in the Word of God. One of the delightful parts of this book is his emphasis on I John 5:14, 15. He quotes this verse as it applied to the baptism of the Holy Spirit, "And this is the confidence we have in him, that if we ask anything according to his will, he heareth us. And we know that if he hear us, we have the petitions we desire of him."

"The entrance into the baptism of the Holy Spirit," Torrey says, "is granted to those who truly repent, identify themselves with Jesus Christ in full surrender, and take Christ at His word." He says that

The Baptism with the Holy Spirit

any child of God may ask Jesus Christ
for the Holy Spirit with the full knowledge
that this is the will of God. If we know
that it is His will, we also may know that
we have (not will have) but *have* the petitions we desire of Him and that the Holy
Spirit will manifest Himself in the life of
the believer and give him power to witness
for Christ.

This new edition gives sound teaching
in this period when the emphasis on the
Holy Spirit is perhaps stronger than in any
other time since Apostolic days. We believe
it provides a scriptural basis for the ever-
widening charismatic movement within the
church. Torrey points out that any movement of the Holy Spirit, from God's standpoint, is meant to make us proper witnesses
of Christ in this world, so that men might
hear the Gospel preached in the power of
the Holy Spirit sent down from heaven.

Harold J. Brokke

Contents

". . . It is quite possible to have something, yes much, of the Spirit's presence and work in the heart and yet come short of that special fullness and work known in the Bible as the baptism or filling with the Holy Spirit."

—R. A. Torrey

"Some of our readers may take exception to Dr. Torrey's use of the term, 'the baptism with the Holy Ghost.' Perhaps if Dr. Torrey lived in our day and saw some of the wildfire in connection with that expression, he would use some other phrase. But let no one quibble about an experience as important as the filling with the Spirit. In this little book, Dr. Torrey quotes Mr. Moody as saying, in a discussion of this very matter, 'Oh, why will they split hairs? Why don't they see that this is just the one thing that they themselves need? They are good teachers, they are wonderful teachers, and I am so glad to have them here, but why will they not see that the baptism with the Holy Ghost is just the one touch that they themselves need?' "

—Will H. Houghton in
Why God Used D. L. Moody

Introduction

It was a great turning point in my ministry when, after much thought and study and meditation, I became satisfied that the baptism with the Holy Spirit was an experience for today and for me, and set myself to obtain it. Such blessing came to me personally that I began giving Bible readings on the subject, and I have continued to do so with increasing frequency as the years have passed. God in His wondrous grace has so greatly blessed these readings and so many have asked for them in printed form, convenient for circulation among their friends, that I decided to write them out in full for publication. It is an occasion of great joy that so many and such excellent books on the person and work of the Holy Spirit have appeared. I wish to call special attention to two of these: *Through the Eternal Spirit* by James Elder Cumming and *The Spirit of Christ* by Andrew Murray.

In the following pages I speak uniformly

of the Holy Spirit, but in the quotations
from the Bible I retain the less desirable
phraseology there used—"the Holy Ghost"
—except in those instances where the trans-
lators themselves varied their usage. Prob-
ably most of the readers of this book already know that "the Holy Spirit" and "the
Holy Ghost" are simply two different trans-
lations of precisely the same Greek words.
It seems very unfortunate, and almost un-
accountable, that the English revisers did
not follow the suggestion of the American
Committee and adopt uniformly the render-
ing "Holy Spirit" for "Holy Ghost."

1

The Baptism with the Holy Spirit:
What It Is and What It Does

While a great deal is said in these days concerning the baptism with the Holy Spirit, it is to be feared that there are many who talk about it and pray for it who have no clear and definite idea of what it is. But the Bible, if carefully studied, will give us a view of this wondrous blessing that is perfectly clear and remarkably definite.

1. We find first of all that *there are a number of designations in the Bible for this one experience.* In Acts 1:5 Jesus said: "Ye shall be baptized with the Holy Ghost not many days hence." In Acts 2:4, when this promise was fulfilled, we read, "They were all filled with the Holy Ghost." In Acts 1:4 the same experience is spoken of as "the promise of the Father," and in Luke 24:49 as "the promise of my Father" and "endued with power from on high." By a comparison of Acts 10:44, 45, and 47 with

Acts 11:15, and 16, we find that the expressions "the Holy Ghost fell on them" and "the gift of the Holy Ghost" and "received the Holy Ghost" are all equivalent to "baptized with the Holy Ghost."

2. We find in the next place that *the baptism with the Holy Spirit is a definite experience* which one may know whether he has received or not. This is evident from our Saviour's command to the apostles: "Tarry ye in the city . . . until ye be endued with power from on high" (Luke 24:49). If this enduement with power, the baptism with the Holy Spirit, were not an experience so definite that one could know whether he had received it or not, how could they tell when those commanded days of tarrying were at an end?

The same thing is clear from Paul's very definite question to the disciples at Ephesus. "Did ye receive the Holy Spirit when ye believed?" (Acts 19:2, ASV). Paul evidently expected a definite "yes" or a definite "no" for an answer. Unless the experience were definite and of such a character that one could know whether he had received it or not, how could these disciples answer Paul's question! In fact, they knew they had not received or been baptized with the Holy Spirit, and a short time afterward they knew they had received and been baptized with the Holy Spirit (Acts 19:6).

Ask many a man today who prays that he may be baptized with the Holy Spirit: "Well, my brother, did you get what you asked—were you baptized with the Holy Spirit?" and he would be dumbfounded. He did not expect anything so definite that he could answer positively yes or no to a question like that.

But we find in the Bible nothing of that vagueness and indefiniteness which we find in much of our modern prayer and speech regarding this subject. The Bible is a very definite book. It is very definite about salvation—so definite that a man who knows his Bible can say positively yes or no to the question, "Are you saved?" The Bible is equally definite about the baptism with the Holy Spirit, so that a man who knows his Bible can say positively yes or no to the question, "Have you been baptized with the Holy Spirit?"

There may be those who are saved who do not know it because they do not understand their Bibles, but it is their privilege to know it. Likewise there may be those who have been baptized with the Holy Spirit who do not know the Bible name for what has come to them, but it is their privilege to know.

3. *The baptism with the Holy Spirit is a work of the Holy Spirit separate and distinct from His regenerating work.* To be regenerated by the Holy Spirit is one thing; to be baptized with the Holy Spirit is something different, something further. This is evident from Acts 1:5. There Jesus said, "Ye shall be baptized with the Holy Ghost *not many days hence.*" They were not then as yet baptized with the Holy Spirit. But they were *already* regenerated. Jesus himself had already pronounced them so. In John 15:3, He said to the same men, "Now ye are clean through the word" (cf. James 1:18; I Pet. 1:23). And in John 13:10: "Ye are clean, but not all," excepting by the "but not all" the one unregenerate man in the apostolic company, Judas Iscariot. (See John 13:11). The apostles, excepting Judas Iscariot, were then already regenerate men, but they were not yet baptized with the Holy Spirit.

From this it is evident that regeneration is one thing and the baptism with the Holy Spirit is something different, something further. One can be regenerated and still not be baptized with the Holy Spirit. The same thing is evident from Acts 8:12-16. Here we find a company of believers who had been baptized. Surely in this company of baptized believers there were some regenerate men. But the record informs us that when Peter and John came down they "prayed for them, that they might receive the Holy Ghost: (*for as yet he was fallen upon none of them*)."

It is clear then that one may be a believer, may be a regenerate man, and yet not have the baptism with the Holy Spirit. In other words, the baptism with the Holy Spirit is something distinct from and beyond His regenerating work. Not every regenerate man has the baptism with the Holy Spirit; though, as we shall see later, every regenerate man may have this baptism. If a man has experienced the regenerating work of the Holy Spirit he is a saved man, but he is not fitted for service until in addition to this he has received the baptism with the Holy Spirit.

4. *The baptism with the Holy Spirit is always connected with testimony and service.* Look carefully at every passage in which the baptism with the Holy Spirit is

mentioned and you will see it is connected with and is for the purpose of testimony and service (for example, Acts 1:5, 8; 2:4; 4: 31, 33). This will come out very clearly when we come to consider what the baptism with the Holy Spirit does. The baptism of the Holy Spirit is not for the purpose of cleansing from sin, but for the purpose of empowering for service.

There is a line of teaching, put forward by a very earnest but mistaken body of people, that has brought the whole doctrine of the baptism with the Holy Spirit into disrepute. It runs this way: First proposition —there is a further experience (or second blessing) after regeneration—namely, the baptism with the Holy Spirit. This proposition is true and can be easily proved from the Bible. Second proposition—this baptism with the Holy Spirit can be instantaneously received. This proposition is also true and can be easily proved from the Bible. Third proposition—this baptism with the Holy Spirit is the eradication of the sinful nature. This proposition is untrue. Not a line of Scripture can be adduced to show that the baptism with the Holy Spirit is the eradication of the sinful nature. The conclusion drawn from these three propositions, two true and one false, is necessarily false.

The baptism with the Holy Spirit is not for the purpose of cleansing from sin, but for the purpose of empowering for service. It is indeed the work of the Holy Spirit to cleanse from sin. Further than this there is a work of the Holy Spirit where the believer is strengthened with might in the inner man, that Christ may dwell in his heart by faith, that he might be filled unto all the fullness of God (Eph. 3:16-19, ASV).

There is a work of the Holy Spirit of such a character that the believer is "made . . . free from the law of sin and death" (Rom. 8:2), and through the Spirit does "mortify [put to death] the deeds of the body" (Rom. 8:13). It is our privilege to so walk daily and hourly in the power of the Spirit, that the carnal nature is kept in the place of death. But this is not the baptism with the Spirit; neither is it the *eradication* of a sinful nature. It is not something done once and for all; it is something that must be momentarily maintained. "*Walk* in the Spirit, and ye shall not fulfill the lust of the flesh" (Gal. 5:16). While insisting that the baptism with the Spirit is primarily for the purpose of empowering for service, it should be added that the baptism is accompanied by a great moral uplift. (See Acts 2:44-46; 4:31-35.) This is necessarily so, from the steps one must take to obtain this blessing.

5. We will get a still clearer and fuller view of what the baptism with the Holy Spirit is if we will notice what this baptism does. This is stated concisely in Acts 1:8: "Ye shall receive *power,* after that the Holy Ghost is come upon you: and ye shall be witnesses. . . ." *The baptism with the Holy Spirit imparts power, power for service.*

This power will not manifest itself in precisely the same way in each individual. This is brought out very clearly in I Corinthians 12:4, 8-11, ASV. "Now there are diversities of gifts, but the same Spirit. . . . For to one is given through the Spirit the word of wisdom; and to another the word of knowledge, according to the same Spirit: to another faith, in the same Spirit; and to another gifts of healings, in the one Spirit . . . to another divers kinds of tongues . . . but all these worketh the one and the same Spirit, dividing to each one severally even as he will."

In my early study of the baptism with

the Holy Spirit, I noticed that in the Scripture, in many instances, those who were so baptized "spoke with tongues." The question came often to my mind, "If one is baptized with the Holy Spirit, will he not speak with tongues?" But I saw no one so speaking and I often wondered, "Is there anyone today who actually is baptized with the Holy Spirit?" This twelfth chapter of I Corinthians cleared me up on that, especially when I found Paul asking of those who had been baptized with the Holy Spirit, "Do all speak with tongues?" (I Cor. 12:30).

But I fell into another error—namely, that anyone who received the baptism with the Holy Spirit would receive power as an evangelist or as a preacher of the Word. This is equally contrary to the teaching of the chapter, that "there are *diversities of gifts,* but the same Spirit."

There are three evils arising from the mistake just mentioned. First, *disappointment.* Many will seek the baptism with the Holy Spirit, expecting power as an evangelist, but God has not called them to that work and the power that comes from the baptism with the Holy Spirit manifests itself in another way to them. Many cases of bitter disappointment and almost despair have arisen from this cause.

The second evil is graver than the first: *presumption.* A man whom God has not called to the work of an evangelist or minister rushes into it because he has received, or thinks he has received, the baptism with the Holy Spirit. Many a man has said, "All a man needs to succeed as a preacher is the baptism with the Holy Spirit." This is not true; he needs a call to that specific work, and he needs the study of the Word of God that will prepare him for the work.

The third evil is still greater: *indifference.* There are many who know they are not called to the work of preaching. For example, a mother with a large family of children knows this. If then, they think that the baptism with the Holy Spirit simply imparts power to preach, it is a matter of no personal concern to them. But when we come to see the truth that while the baptism with the Spirit imparts power, the way in which that power will be manifested depends upon the work to which God has called us and no efficient work can be done without it. Then the mother will see that she equally with the preacher needs this baptism—needs it for that most important and hallowed of all work, to bring up her children "in the nurture and admonition of the Lord."

I have recently met a very happy mother. A few months ago she heard of the baptism with the Holy Spirit, sought it and received it. "Oh," she joyfully exclaimed as she told me the story, "since I received it, I have been able to get into the hearts of my children which I was never able to do before."

It is the Holy Spirit himself who decides how the power will manifest itself in any given case; "the same Spirit dividing to each one severally even as *he* will" (I Cor. 12:11, ASV). We have a right to "desire earnestly the greater gifts" (I Cor. 12:31), but the Holy Spirit is sovereign, and He, not we, must determine in the final issue. It is not for us then to select some gift and look to the Holy Spirit to impart the self-chosen gift. It is not for us to select some field of service and then look to the Holy Spirit to impart to us power in the field which *we* have chosen. It is rather for us to recognize the divinity and sovereignty of the Spirit, and to put ourselves unreservedly at His disposal. It is for Him to select

the gift that "he will" and impart to us that
gift; it is for Him to select for us the field
that "he will" and impart to us the power
that will qualify us for the field He has
chosen.

I once knew a child of God who, hearing
of the baptism with the Holy Spirit and the
power that resulted from it, gave up at a
great sacrifice the secular work in which
he was engaged and entered upon the work
of an evangelist. But the expected power
in that line did not follow. The man fell into
great doubt and darkness until he was led
to see that the Holy Spirit divideth "to
each one severally even as he will." Then
giving up selecting his own field and gifts,
he put himself at the Holy Spirit's disposal
for Him to choose. In the final outcome the
Holy Spirit did impart to this man power
as an evangelist and a preacher of the
Word. We must then surrender ourselves
absolutely to the Holy Spirit to work as He
will.

But while the power that the baptism
with the Holy Spirit brings manifests itself
in different ways in different individuals,
there will always be power. Just as surely
as a man is baptized with the Holy Spirit,
there will be new power, a power not his
own, the power of the Highest!

Religious biography abounds in instances of men who have worked along as best they could until one day they were led to see there was such an experience as the baptism with the Holy Spirit and to seek it and obtain it; from that hour there came into their service a new power that utterly transformed its character. Finney, Brainerd, and Moody are cases in point. But cases of this character are not confined to a few exceptional men. The author has personally met and corresponded with those who could testify to the new power that God granted them through the baptism with the Holy Spirit. These hundreds of men and women were in all branches of Christian service. Many of them were ministers of the gospel, mission workers, YMCA secretaries, Sunday school teachers, personal workers, fathers and mothers. Nothing could exceed the clearness, confidence, and joyfulness of many of these testimonies. What we have in promise in the words of Christ many have, and all may have, in glad experience: "Ye shall receive power, after that the Holy Ghost is come upon you."

To sum up the contents of this chapter: The baptism with the Holy Spirit is the Spirit of God coming upon the believer, taking possession of his faculties, imparting to him gifts not naturally his own but which qualify him for the service to which God has called him.

2

The Necessity and Possibility
of the
Baptism with the Holy Spirit

Shortly before Christ was received up into heaven, having committed the preaching of the gospel to His disciples, He laid upon them this very solemn charge concerning the beginning of the great work He had committed to their hands: "Behold, I send forth the promise of my Father upon you: but tarry ye in the city, until ye be clothed with power from on high" (Luke 24:49, ASV). There is no doubt as to what Jesus meant by the "promise of my Father" for which they were to wait before beginning the ministry which He had entrusted to them, for in Acts 1:4 and 5, ASV, we read that Jesus "charged them not to depart from Jerusalem, but to wait for the promise of the Father, which, said he, ye heard from me: for John indeed baptized with water; but ye shall be baptized

in the Holy Spirit not many days hence."
"The promise of the Father," through
which the enduement of power was to come,
was the baptism with the Holy Spirit (cf.
Acts 1:8). Christ then strictly charged His
disciples not to presume to undertake the
work to which He had called them until they
had received as the necessary and all-
essential preparation for that work, the
baptism with the Holy Spirit.

The men to whom Jesus said this seemed
to have already received very thorough
preparation for the work in hand. They had
been to school with Christ himself for more
than three years. They had heard from His
own lips the great truths that they were to
proclaim to the world. They had been eyewitnesses of His miracles, of His death,
and of His resurrection, and were about to
be eyewitnesses of His ascension. The work
before them was simply to go forth to proclaim what their own eyes had seen and
what their own ears had heard from the
lips of Christ himself. Were they not fully
prepared for this work? It would seem so
to us. But Christ said, "No, you are so utterly unprepared you must not stir a step
yet.

"There is a further preparation, so all-essential to effective service, you must abide at Jerusalem until you receive it. This further preparation is the baptism with the Holy Spirit. When you receive that— and *not until then*—you will be prepared to begin the work to which I have called you." If Christ did not permit these men, who had received so rare and unparalleled a schooling for the work to which He had so definitely and clearly called them—if He did not permit them to undertake this work without receiving, in addition, the baptism with the Holy Spirit, what is it for us to undertake the work to which He has called us until we have received the baptism with the Holy Spirit? Is it not most daring presumption?

But this is not all. In Acts 10:38 we read "how God anointed Jesus of Nazareth with the Holy Ghost and with power: who went about doing good, and healing all that were oppressed of the devil." When we look into the Gospels for an explanation of these words, we find it in Luke 3:21, 22; 4:1, 14, 15, 18, and 21. We find that at the baptism of Jesus at Jordan, as He prayed the Holy Spirit come upon Him. Then "full of the Holy Ghost" He had the temptation experience. Then "in the power of the Spirit" He begins His ministry and proclaims himself "anointed to preach" because "the Spirit of the Lord is upon me." In other words, Jesus the Christ never entered upon the ministry for which He came into this world until He was baptized with the Holy Spirit.

If Jesus Christ, who had been supernaturally conceived through the Holy Spirit's power, who was the only begotten Son of God, who was divine, very God of very God and yet truly man—if He, "leaving us an example that we should follow in his steps," did not venture upon the ministry for which the Father had sent Him until thus baptized with the Holy Spirit, what is it for us to dare to do it? If, in the light of these recorded facts, we dare to do it, it seems like an offense going beyond presumption. Doubtless it has been done in ignorance by many, but can we plead ignorance any longer? The baptism with the Holy Spirit is an absolutely necessary preparation for effective service for Christ along every line of service.

We may have a very clear call to service; it may be as clear as the apostles had —but the charge is laid upon us, as upon them, that before we begin that service we must "tarry until ye be clothed with power from on high." This enduement with power is through the baptism with the Holy Spirit.

There are certainly few greater mistakes being made today than that of setting men to teach Sunday school classes, do personal work, and even preach the gospel, simply because they have been converted and have received a certain amount of education—perhaps including a college and seminary course—but without having been as yet baptized with the Holy Spirit. Any man who is in Christian work who has not received the baptism with the Holy Spirit ought to stop his work right where he is and not go on with it until he has been "clothed with power from on high."

But what will our work do while we are waiting? What did the world do those ten days while the early disciples were waiting? They alone knew the saving truth; yet in obedience to the Lord's command, they were silent. The world was no loser. When the power came they accomplished more in one day than they would have accomplished in years if they had gone on in presumptuous disobedience to Christ's charge. We also, after we have received the baptism with the Holy Spirit, will accomplish more in one day than we ever would in years without His power. Days spent in waiting, if it were necessary, would be well spent; but we shall see further on that there is no need that we spend days in waiting.

It may be said that the apostles had gone out on missionary tours during Christ's lifetime before they were baptized with the Holy Spirit. This is true, but that was before the Holy Spirit was given and before the charge, "Tarry . . . until ye be clothed with power from on high." After that it would have been disobedience and presumption to have gone forth without this enduement; we are living today after the Holy Spirit has been given and after the charge to "tarry . . . until . . . clothed."

We come now to the question of the possibility of the baptism with the Holy Spirit. Is the baptism with the Holy Spirit for us? This is a question that has a plain and explicit answer in the Word of God. In Acts 2:39 (ASV) we read: "For to you is the promise, and to your children, and to all that are afar off, even as many as the Lord our God shall call unto him."

What is the promise of this passage? Turning back to verses 4 and 5 of the pre-

ceding chapter we read: "Wait for the
promise of the Father, which, saith he, ye
have heard of me. For John truly baptized
with water; but ye shall be baptized with
the Holy Ghost not many days hence."
Again in Acts 2:33 we read: "Having received of the Father the promise of the
Holy Ghost."

It would seem to be perfectly clear that
the promise of verse 39 must be the same
as the promise of verse 33 and verses 4 and
5 of the preceding chapter—the promise of
the baptism with the Holy Spirit. This conclusion is rendered absolutely certain by
the context: "Repent ye, and be baptized
every one of you in the name of Jesus Christ
unto the remission of your sins; and ye shall
receive the gift of the Holy Spirit. For to
you is the promise...." The promise of
this verse, then, is the promise of the gift
or baptism with the Holy Spirit. (Cf. Acts
10:45 with Acts 11:15, 16.)

Whom is this gift for? "To you," says
Peter to the Jews whom he was immediately addressing. Then looking over their
heads to the next generation, "And to your
children." Then looking down all the coming ages of the Church's history to Gentile
as well as Jew: "And to all that are afar

off, even as many as the Lord our God shall call unto him." The baptism with the Holy Spirit is for every child of God in every age of the Church's history. If it is not ours in experimental possession, it is because we have not taken what God has provided for us in our exalted Saviour (the exact force of the word *receive* in verse 38 is *take*—Acts 2:33; John 7:38, 39).

A minister of the gospel came to me after a lecture on the baptism with the Holy Spirit and said: "The church to which I belong teaches that the baptism with the Holy Spirit was for the apostolic ages alone."

"It matters not," was replied, "what the church to which you belong or the church to which I belong teaches. What says the Word of God?"

Acts 2:39 was read: "To you is the promise, and to your children, and to all that are afar off, even as many as the Lord our God shall call unto him."

"Has He called you?" I asked.

"Yes, He certainly has."

"Is the promise for you?"

"Yes, it is."

And it was. And it is for every child of God who reads these pages. What a thrilling thought it is that the baptism with the Holy Spirit, the enduement with *power from on high*, is for us, is for *me* as an individual.

But that unspeakable joyous thought has its solemn side. If I may be baptized with the Holy Spirit, I *must* be. If I am baptized with the Holy Spirit, then will souls be saved through my instrumentality who would not be saved if I were not so baptized. If then I am not willing to pay the price of this baptism, and therefore am not so baptized, I am responsible before God for all the souls that might have been saved but were not saved through me.

I oftentime tremble for my brethren and myself in Christian work. Not because we are teaching deadly error to men—some are guilty of even that, but I do not refer to that now; not that we are not teaching the full truth as it is in Jesus—it must be confessed that there are many who do not teach positive error who do not preach a full gospel, but I do not refer to that. I tremble for those who are preaching the truth—the truth as it is in Jesus, the gospel in its simplicity, in its purity, in its fullness —but preaching it "in persuasive words of wisdom" and not "in demonstration of the Spirit and of power" (I Cor. 2:4, ASV),

preaching it in the energy of the flesh and
not in the power of the Holy Spirit. There
is nothing more deadly than the gospel without the Spirit's power. "The letter killeth,
but the Spirit giveth life."

It is awfully solemn business preaching
the gospel either from the pulpit or in quiet-
er ways. It means death or life to those
who hear; and whether it means death or
life depends very largely on whether we
preach it without or with the baptism with
the Holy Spirit. We must be baptized with
the Holy Spirit.

It is sometimes argued that the baptism
with the Holy Spirit was for the purpose
of imparting miracle-working power and
for the apostolic age alone. In favor of this
position it is asserted that the baptism with
the Holy Spirit was followed quite uniformly
by miracles. The untenableness of this position is seen: (1) By the fact Christ himself
asserted that the purpose of the baptism
with the Holy Spirit was to impart power
for witnessing—not especially power to
work miracles (Acts 1:5, 8; Luke 24:48, 49).
(2) By the fact that Paul distinctly taught
that there were diversities of gifts, and that
"workings of miracles" was only one of the
manifestations of the baptism with the Holy

Spirit (I Cor. 12:4, 8-10). (3) By the fact that Peter distinctly asserts that "the gift of the Holy Ghost," the promise, is for all believers in all generations (Acts 2:38, 39). It is evident from a comparison of Acts 2:39 with Luke 24:49; Acts 1:4, 5; 2:33; and of Acts 2:38 with Acts 10:45 and Acts 11:15, 16, that each of these two expressions, *the promise*, and *the gift of the Holy Ghost*, refers to the baptism with the Holy Spirit.

If we take miracles in a broad sense of all results wrought by supernatural power, then it is true that each one baptized with the Holy Spirit does receive miracle-working power; for each one so baptized does receive a power not naturally his own—supernatural power, God's own power. The result of the baptism with the Holy Spirit that was most noticeable and essential was convincing, convicting, and converting power (Acts 2:4, 37, 41; 4:8-13, 31, 33; 9:17, 20-22). There seem to have been no displays of miracle-working power immediately following Paul's baptism with the Holy Spirit, even though he became so singularly gifted in this direction at a later day; it was power to witness for Jesus, the Son of God, that he received in immediate connection with the baptism with the Holy Spirit.

3

How the Baptism with the Holy Spirit
Can Be Obtained

We have now come to a place where there
is a deep sense that we must be baptized
with the Holy Spirit. The practical question
confronts us: how can we obtain this baptism with the Holy Spirit which we so sorely
need? The Word of God also answers this
question very plainly and very explicitly.
There is pointed out in the Bible a path con-
sisting of seven simple steps, which anyone
who will can take, and whoever takes these
seven steps will, with absolute certainty,
enter into this blessing. This statement may
seem very positive, but the Word of God
is equally positive regarding the outcome
of taking these steps which it points out.

All seven steps are stated or implied in
Acts 2:38: "Repent ye, and be baptized
every one of you in the name of Jesus Christ
unto the remission of your sins; *and ye shall
receive* the gift of the Holy Spirit."

The first three steps are brought out with special definiteness and distinctness in this verse. The others which are clearly implied in the verse are brought out more explicitly by other passages to which we shall refer later.

1. The first two steps are found in the word *repent*. What does "repent" mean? It means to *change your mind*. Change your mind about what? About God, about Christ, about sin. As to what change of mind is about in any given case must be determined by the context. Here the first and most prominent thought is a change of mind about Christ. Peter has just brought against his hearers the awful charge that they had crucified Him whom God had made both Lord and Christ. "Pricked in their heart" by this charge, carried home by the power of the Holy Spirit, his hearers had cried out: "Men and brethren, what shall we do?" "Repent," Peter answered. Change your mind about Christ. Change from a Christ-hating and Christ-crucifying attitude of mind to a Christ-accepting attitude of mind. Accept Jesus as Christ and Lord. This then is the first step toward the baptism with the Holy Spirit: Accept Jesus as Christ and Lord.

2. The second step is also found in the word *repent*. While the change of mind about Jesus is the first and prominent thought, there must also be a change of mind about sin—a change of mind from a sin-loving or sin-indulging attitude to a sin-hating and sin-renouncing attitude. This is the second step: *renounce sin*, all sin, every sin.

Here we come upon one of the most common obstacles to receiving the Holy Spirit—sin. Something is held on to that in our inmost hearts we more or less definitely feel to be not pleasing to God. If we are to receive the Holy Spirit, there must be very honest and very thorough heart searching. We cannot do satisfactory searching ourselves; God must do it. If we wish to receive the Holy Spirit, we should go alone with God and ask Him to search us thoroughly and bring to light anything that displeases Him (Ps. 139:23, 24). Then we should wait for Him to do it. When the displeasing thing is revealed, it should be put away at once. If, after patient and honest waiting, nothing is brought to light, we may conclude there is nothing of this kind in the way, and proceed to the further steps. But we should not conclude this too hurriedly. The sin that hinders the blessing may be something that appears very small and insignificant in itself.

Mr. Finney tells of a young woman who was deeply concerned regarding the baptism with the Holy Spirit. Night after night she agonized in prayer, but the desired blessing did not come. One night as she was in prayer there came up before her some matter of head adornment that had often troubled her before; putting her hand to her head, she took the pins out and threw them away and immediately the blessing came. This was a small matter in itself, a matter that would not have appeared to many as sin, but yet a matter of controversy between this woman and God; and when this was settled the blessing came. "Whatsoever is not of faith is sin" (Rom. 14:23), and it matters not how little the thing may be; if there are questions regarding it, it must be put away if we are to have the baptism with the Holy Spirit. The second step then toward the baptism with the Holy Spirit is to put away every sin.

3. The third step is found in this same verse: "Be baptized in the name of Jesus Christ unto the remission of your sins." It was immediately after His baptism that the

Holy Spirit descended upon Jesus (Luke 3:21, 22). In His baptism Jesus, though himself sinless, humbled himself to take the sinner's place, and then God highly exalted Him by the giving of the Holy Spirit and by the audible testimony: "Thou art my beloved Son; in thee I am well pleased." So we must humble ourselves to make open confession of our sin and renounce it and accept Jesus Christ in God's appointed way, *by baptism*. The baptism with the Holy Spirit is not for the one who secretly takes his place as a sinner and believer in Christ, but for the one who does so openly. Of course, the baptism with the Holy Spirit may precede water baptism as in the case of the household of Cornelius (Acts 10:47). But this was evidently an exceptional case and water baptism immediately followed. I have little doubt that there have been those among Christians who did not believe in or practice water baptism—as for example the Friends or Quakers—who have had and have given evidence of the baptism with the Holy Spirit, but the passage before us certainly presents the normal order.

4. The fourth step is clearly implied in the verse we have been studying (Acts 2:38), but it is brought out more explicitly in Acts

5:32: "The Holy Ghost, whom God hath
given to them that obey him." The fourth
step is *obedience*.

What does obedience mean? It does not
mean merely doing some of the things or
many of the things or most of the things
that God bids us do. It means *total surrender to the will of God*. Obedience is an
attitude of the will lying back of specific
acts of obedience. It means that I come
to God and say: "Heavenly Father, here
I am and all I have. Thou hast bought me
with a price and I acknowledge Thine absolute ownership. Take me and all I have,
and do with me whatsoever Thou wilt. Send
me where Thou wilt; use me as Thou wilt.
I surrender myself and all I possess absolutely, unconditionally, forever to Thy con-
trol and use."

It was when the burnt offering—*whole*,
no part held back—was laid on the altar
that "there came forth fire from before the
Lord" and accepted the gift (Lev. 9:24),
and it is when we bring ourselves, a *whole*
burnt offering, to the Lord and lay ourselves
thus upon the altar that fire comes and God
accepts the gift. Here we touch upon the
hindrance to the baptism with the Holy Spirit in many lives: there is not total sur-

render; the will is not laid down; the heart
does not cry, "Lord, where Thou wilt, what
Thou wilt, as Thou wilt." One man desires
the baptism with the Holy Spirit that he
may preach or work with power in Boston,
when God wishes him in Bombay. Another,
that he may preach to popular audiences,
when God wishes him to plod among the
poor.

A young woman at a convention ex-
pressed a strong desire that someone would
speak on the baptism with the Holy Spirit.
The address went home with power to her
heart. She had been for some time in deep
travail of soul when I asked her what it
was that she desired.

"Oh," she cried, "I cannot go back to
Baltimore until I am baptized with the Holy
Spirit."

"Is your will laid down?"

"I don't know."

"You wish to go back to Baltimore to
be a Christian worker?"

"Yes."

"Are you willing to go back to Baltimore
and be a servant girl if that is where God
wishes you?"

"No, I am not."

"Well, you will never get the baptism

with the Holy Spirit until you are. Will you lay your will down?"

"I can't."

"Are you willing God should lay it down for you?"

"Yes."

"Well, then ask Him to do it." The head was bowed in brief but earnest prayer. "Did God hear that prayer?"

"He must have; it was according to His will. He did."

"Now ask Him for the baptism with the Holy Spirit." Again the head was bowed and the brief, earnest prayer ascended to God. There was a short silence and the agony was over; the blessing had come—when the will was surrendered.

There are many who hold back from this total surrender because they fear God's will. They are afraid God's will may be something dreadful. Remember who God is; He is our Father. Never an earthly father had so loving and tender a will regarding his children as God has toward us. "No good thing will he withhold from them that walk uprightly" (Ps. 84:11). "He that spared not his own Son, but delivered him up for us all, how shall he not with him also freely give us all things?" There is nothing to be feared in God's will. God's will will always prove in the final outcome the best and sweetest thing in all God's universe.

5. The fifth step is found in Luke 11:13: "If ye then, being evil, know how to give good gifts unto your children: how much more shall your heavenly Father give the Holy Spirit to them that ask him?" The asking of this verse is the asking that springs from *real and intense desire*. This is brought out by the context: "Ask, and it shall be given you; seek, and ye shall find; knock, and it shall be opened unto you." Note also the parable of the importunate friend that immediately precedes. Evidently the asking that Christ has in mind is not the asking of a passing and halfhearted whim, but the asking of intense desire.

There is a very suggestive passage in Isaiah 44:3: "I will pour water upon him that is *thirsty* .... I will pour my spirit upon thy seed." What does it mean to be thirsty? When one is thirsty there is but one cry: "Water! Water! Water!" Every pore in the body seems to have a voice and cries out, "Water!" So when our hearts have one cry, "The Holy Spirit, the Holy Spirit, the Holy Spirit," then it is that God pours floods upon the dry ground, pours His Spirit upon us. This then is the fifth step—intense desire for the baptism with the Holy Spirit. To what a pitch of longing the early disciples had been brought by the tenth day of their eager waiting, and their thirsty souls were filled that day when "Pentecost was fully come"! As long as one thinks he can get along somehow without the baptism with the Holy Spirit, as long as he casts about for something in the way of education or cunningly concocted methods of work, he is not going to receive it.

There are many ministers who are missing the fullness of power God has for them simply because they are not willing to admit the lack there has been all these years in their ministry. It is indeed a humiliating thing to confess, but that humiliating confession would be the precursor of a marvelous blessing. But there are not a few who, in their unwillingness to make this wholesome confession, are casting about for some ingenious device or exegesis to get around the plain and simple meaning of God's Word, and thus they are cheating themselves of the fullness of the Spirit's power that God is so eager to bestow upon them.

And furthermore, they are imperiling the eternal interests of the souls that are dependent upon this ministrations, that might be won for Christ if they had the power of the Holy Spirit which they might have.

There are others whom God in His grace has brought to see that there was a something their ministry lacked, and this something is nothing less than that all-essential baptism with the Holy Spirit, without which one is utterly unqualified for acceptable and effective service. And they have humbly and frankly confessed their lack; sometimes they have been led to the God-taught resolution that they would not go on in their work until this lack was supplied. They have waited in eager longing upon God the Father for the fulfillment of His promise, and the result has been a transformed ministry for which many have risen to bless God.

It is not enough that the desire for the baptism with the Holy Spirit be intense; it must also have the right motive. There is a desire for the baptism with the Holy Spirit that is purely selfish. There is many a one who has an intense desire for the baptism with the Holy Spirit simply that he may be a great preacher, or great per-

sonal worker, or renowned in some way
as a Christian. It is simply his own gain
or glory that he is seeking. After all, it
is not the Holy Spirit whom he seeks, but
his own honor and the baptism with the
Holy Spirit is simply a means to that end.
One of the most subtle and dangerous
snares into which Satan leads us is seeking
the Holy Spirit, this most solemn of all gifts,
for our own ends.

The desire for the Holy Spirit must not
be in order to make that sublime and divine
person the servant of our low ends, but for
the glory of God. It must arise from a recog-
nition that God and Christ are being dishonored by my powerless ministry and by
the sin of the people about me, against
which I have no power, and that He will
be honored if I have the baptism with the
Spirit of God.

One of the most solemn passages in the
New Testament bears upon this point.
"When Simon saw that through the laying
on of the apostles' hands the Holy Spirit
was given, he offered them money, saying,
Give me also this power, that on whomso-
ever I lay my hands, he may receive the
Holy Spirit" (Acts 8:18-24, ASV). Here was
a strong desire on Simon's part, but it was

entirely unhallowed and selfish, and Peter's
terrific answer is worthy of note and meditation. Is there not many a one today who,
with equally unhallowed and selfish purpose, desires the baptism with the Holy
Spirit? Each one, who is desiring and seeking the baptism with the Holy Spirit, would
do well to ask himself *why* he desires it.
If you find that it is merely for your own
gratification or glory, then ask God to for-
give you the thought of your heart, and to
enable you to see how you need it for His
glory and to desire it to that end.

6. The sixth step is in this same verse
(Luke 11:13). "If ye then, being evil, know
how to give good gifts unto your children:
how much more shall your heavenly Father
give the Holy Spirit to them that ask him?"
The sixth step is *to ask*—definite asking
for a definite blessing. When Christ has
been accepted as Saviour and Master, and
confessed as such; when sin has been put
away; when there has been the definite,
total surrender of the will; when there is
real and holy desire—then comes the simple
act of asking God for this definite blessing.
It is given in answer to earnest, definite,
specific, believing prayer.

It has been earnestly contended by some

that we should not pray for the Holy Spirit. They reason it out in this way: "The Holy Spirit was given to the Church at Pentecost, as an abiding gift." This is true, but what was given to the Church must be appropriated by each believer for himself. It has been well said on this point that God has already given Christ to the world (John 3:16), but that each individual must appropriate Him by a personal act to get the personal advantage of the gift; and so must each individual personally appropriate God's gift of the Holy Spirit to get the personal advantage of it. But it is argued still further that each believer has the Holy Spirit. This is also true in a sense. "If any man have not the Spirit of Christ, he is none of his" (Rom. 8:9). But as we have already seen, it is quite possible to have something, yes, much, of the Spirit's presence and work in the heart and yet come short of that special fullness and work known in the Bible as the baptism or filling with the Holy Spirit.

In answer to all specious reasonings on this subject we present the simple statement of Christ: "How much more shall your heavenly Father give the Holy Spirit to them that *ask* him?"

At a convention at which the author was announced to speak on this subject, a man said to him, "I see you are to speak on the baptism with the Holy Spirit."

"Yes."

"It is the most important subject on the program; now be sure to tell them not to pray for the Holy Spirit."

"I shall certainly not tell them that; for Jesus said: 'How much more shall your heavenly Father give the Holy Spirit to them that *ask* him?"

"Oh, but that was before Pentecost."

"How about Acts 4:31? Was that before Pentecost or after?"

"After it, of course."

"Well, read it."

It was read: "When they had *prayed*, the place was shaken where they were assembled together, and they were all filled with the Holy Ghost."

"How about the eighth chapter of Acts? Was that before or after Pentecost?"

"After, of course."

"Well, read verses 14-16."

The verses were read: "Peter and John, when they were come down, prayed for them, that they might receive the Holy Ghost; for as yet he was fallen upon none

lieve that ye [already] *received* them,
and ye *shall have them.*"

This seeming enigma was solved long
after, while studying I John. I read: "This
is the boldness which we have toward him,
that, if we ask anything according to his
will, he heareth us: and if we know that
he heareth us whatsoever we ask, we know
that *we have* the petitions which we have
asked of him" (5:14, 16, ASV). When I ask
anything of God, the first thing to find out
is this: Is this petition according to His
will? When that is settled, when I find
it is according to His will, when, for example, the thing asked is definitely promised in His Word—then I know the prayer
is heard, and I know further "I have the
petition which I have asked of him." I know
it because He plainly says so, and what
I have thus appropriated on simple, child-
like faith in His naked Word I shall have
in actual experience.

When one who has a clear title to a
piece of property deeds it to me, it is mine
as soon as the deed is properly executed
and recorded, though it may be some time
before I enter into the experimental joy
of it. I have it in the one sense as soon
as the deed is recorded. I shall have it

in the other sense later. In like manner, as soon as we, having met the conditions of prevailing prayer, put up to God a petition for anything according to His will, it is our privilege to know that the prayer is heard, and that the thing which we have asked of Him is ours.

Now apply this to the baptism with the Holy Spirit. I have met the conditions for obtaining this blessing already mentioned. I simply, definitely ask God the Father for the baptism with the Holy Spirit. Then I stop and ask, "Was that prayer according to His will?" Yes, Luke 11:13 says so: "If ye then, being evil, know how to give good gifts unto your children: how much more shall your heavenly Father give the Holy Spirit to them that ask him?" Acts 2:38 and 39 says: "Repent ye, and be baptized every one of you in the name of Jesus Christ unto the remission of your sins; and ye shall receive the gift of the Holy Spirit. For to you is the promise, and to your children, and to all that are afar off, even as many as the Lord our God shall call unto him" (ASV). It is clear that the prayer for the baptism with the Holy Spirit is "according to his will," for it is definitely and plainly promised. I know then that the prayer is heard and that *I have the petition which I have asked of him* (I John 5:14, 15, ASV); that is, I have the baptism with the Holy Spirit. I have then the right to arise from my knees and say on the all-sufficient authority of God's Word, "I have the baptism with the Holy Spirit"; and *afterward* I shall have in experimental enjoyment what I have appropriated by simple faith; for God has said, and He cannot lie, "All things whatsoever ye pray and ask for, believe that ye have received them, *and ye shall have them.*"

If Christ has been accepted as Saviour and Lord and openly confessed as such in God's way; if sin has been searched out and put away; if there has been total surrender of the will and of self to God; if there is a true desire, for God's glory, to be baptized with the Holy Spirit—if these conditions have been met, any reader may ask God to baptize him with the Holy Spirit. He can then say, when the prayer has gone up, "That prayer was heard; I have what I have asked; I *have the baptism with the Holy Spirit*"; and he has a right to get up and go out to his work assured that in that work he will have the Holy Spirit's power.

But someone will ask, "Must I not know that I have the baptism with the Holy Spirit before I begin the work?" Certainly, but how shall we know? I know of no better way of knowing than by God's Word. I would believe God's Word before my feelings any day. How do we deal with an inquirer who has accepted Christ but who lacks assurance that he has eternal life? We do not ask him to look at his feelings, but we take him to some passage such as John 3:36.

We tell him to read it and he reads: "He that believeth on the Son hath everlasting life."

"Who says that?" we ask.

"God says it."

"Is it true?"

"Oh, certainly it is true; God says it."

"Who does God say has everlasting life?"

"He that believeth on the Son."

"Do you believe on the Son?"

"Yes."

"What have you then?"

"Oh, I don't know; I don't feel yet that I have eternal life."

"But what does God say?"

"He that believeth on the Son hath everlasting life."

"Are you going to believe God or your feelings?"

We hold the inquirer right there until on the simple, naked Word of God, feeling or no feeling, he says, "I know I have eternal life because God says so," and afterward the feeling comes.

Deal with yourself in this matter of the baptism with the Holy Spirit just as you deal with an inquirer in the matter of assurance. *Be sure you have met the conditions,* and then simply *ask, claim, act.*

But someone will say, "Will it be just as it was before? Won't there be any manifestation?"

Most assuredly there will be some manifestation. "To each one is given the manifestation of the Spirit to profit withal" (I Cor. 12:7, ASV). But what will be the character of the manifestation, and where shall we see it? It is at this point that many make a mistake. They have, perhaps, read the life of Mr. Finney or of Jonathan Edwards, and recall how great waves of electric emotion swept over these men until they were obliged to ask God to withdraw His hand lest they die from the ecstasy. Or they have gone to some meetings and heard testimonies to similar experiences, and they expect something like this.

Now I do not deny the reality of such experiences. I cannot. The testimony of such men as Finney and Edwards is to be believed. There is a stronger reason why I cannot deny them. But while admitting the reality of these experiences, I would ask, "Where is a single line of the New Testament that describes any such experience in connection with the baptism with the Holy Spirit?" Every manifestation of the baptism with the Holy Spirit in the New Testament was in new power in service. Look, for example, at I Corinthians 12 where this subject is treated in a most thorough way, and note the character of the manifestations mentioned. It is quite probable that the apostles had similar experiences to those of Finney and Edwards and others, but if they had, the Holy Spirit kept them from recording them. It is well He did, for if they had told of such things, we would have looked for these things rather than the more important manifestation—power in service.

But another question will be asked: "Did not the apostles wait ten days and may

"Ask Him to." We knelt in prayer, and he asked God to lay down his will for him. "Did God hear that prayer?"

"He must have; it was according to His will."

"Is your will laid down?"

"It must be."

"Then ask God for the baptism with the Holy Spirit." He did this. "Was that prayer according to His will?"

"Yes."

"Was it heard?"

"It must have been."

"Have you the baptism with the Holy Spirit?"

"I don't feel it."

"That is not what I asked you; read those verses again."

The Bible lay open at I John 5:14, 15, and he read: "This is the confidence that we have in him, that, if we ask anything according to his will, he heareth us."

In Acts there was no waiting (Acts 11:15, 16).

"Wait a moment; was that prayer according to His will?"

"It certainly was."

"Was it heard?"

"It was."

"Read on."

"And if we know that he hear us, whatsoever we ask, we know that we have the petitions that we desired of him."

"Know what?"

"That we have the petitions we desired of him."

"What was the petition?"

"The baptism with the Holy Spirit."

"Have you it?"

"I don't feel it, but God says so, and I must have."

A few days later I met him again and asked if he really had received what he took on simple faith.

With a happy look on his face he answered, "Yes."

I lost sight of him for perhaps two years, and then found him preparing for the ministry and already preaching. God was honoring his preaching with souls being saved, and a little later used him with others as a means of great blessing to the theological seminary where he was studying. He had also decided to serve Christ on the foreign field. What he claimed in simple faith and received, anyone can claim and receive in the same way.

4

"Fresh Baptisms" with the
Holy Spirit
or the
Refilling with the Holy Spirit

In Acts 2:4 we read: "They were all filled with the Holy Ghost, and began to speak. . . ." This was the fulfillment of Acts 1:5: "Ye shall be baptized with the Holy Ghost not many days hence." One of those mentioned by name as being "filled with the Holy Ghost" (Acts 2:4) or "baptized with the Holy Ghost" (Acts 1:5) at this time was Peter. In Acts 4:8 we read: "Then Peter, filled with the Holy Ghost, said unto them. . . ." Here Peter experienced a new filling with the Spirit. Again, in verse 31 of this same chapter, we read: "When they had prayed, the place was shaken where they were assembled together; and they were all filled with the Holy Ghost." Peter is named as one of this company (vss. 19,

23), so we see that Peter here experienced a third filling with the Holy Spirit.

It is evident that it is not sufficient that one be once baptized with the Holy Spirit. As new emergencies of service arise, there must be new fillings with the Spirit. The failure to realize this has led to sad and serious results in many a man's service. He has been baptized with the Holy Spirit at some period in his life, and strives to get through his whole future life in the power of this past experience. It is largely for this reason that we see so many men who once unquestionably worked in the Holy Spirit's power, who give little evidence of the possession of that power today. For each new service that is to be conducted, for each new soul that is to be dealt with, for each new service for Christ that is to be performed, for each new day and each new emergency of Christian life and service, we should definitely seek a new filling with the Holy Spirit.

I do not deny that there is an anointing that abideth (I John 2:27), nor the permanency of the gifts that the Holy Spirit bestows. I simply assert with clear and abundant Scripture proof, to say nothing of proof from experience and observation, that this gift must not be neglected (I Tim. 4:14), but rather kindled anew or stirred into a flame (II Tim. 1:6, ASV, marg); and that repeated fillings with the Holy Spirit are necessary to continuance and increase of power.

Now arises the question, "Ought these new *fillings* with the Holy Spirit to be called 'fresh *baptisms*' with the Holy Spirit?" While on the one hand it must be admitted that in Acts 2:4 the expression "*filled with the Holy Ghost*" is used to describe the experience promised in Acts 1:5 in the words: "Ye shall be *baptized* with the Holy Ghost," and that therefore the two expressions are to this extent synonymous; on the other hand, it should be noticed that expression "baptized with the Holy Ghost" is nowhere used in the Bible of any experience but the first, and that furthermore the word *baptized* of itself suggests an initial or initiatory experience. While therefore we stand for the truth as which those who speak of "fresh baptisms with the Holy Spirit" are aiming, it would seem wisest to follow the uniform Bible usage and speak of the experiences that succeed the first

him and he about to be taken into wretched captivity, the sport of the godless, and to die with the enemies of the Lord a violent and dishonored death.

Unfortunately Samson is not the only man in Christian history who, having once known the power of the Holy Spirit, has afterward been shorn of this power and laid aside. There have been many Samsons, and I presume there will be many more—men whom God has once used and has afterward been forced to lay aside. One of the saddest sights on earth is such a man. Let us consider when it is that the Lord departs from a man or withdraws His power from him—in other words, *"How power is lost."*

1. First of all, *God withdraws His power from men when they go back on their separation to Him.* This was the precise case with Samson (Judg. 16:19; cf. Num. 6:2, 5). His uncut hair was the outward sign of his Nazarite vow by which "he separated himself unto the Lord." The shearing of his hair was the surrender of his separation. With his separation given up, he was shorn of his power. It is at this same point that many a man today is shorn of his power. There was a day when he separated himself

unto God. He turned his back utterly upon the world and its ambitions, its spirit, its purposes. He set himself apart to God as holy unto Him, to be His, for God to take him and use him and do with him what He would.

God has honored his separation; He has anointed him with the Holy Ghost and power. He has been used of God.

But Delilah has come to him. The world has captured his heart again. He has listened to the world's siren voice and allowed her to shear him of the sign of separation. He is no longer a man separated, or wholly consecrated to the Lord, and the Lord leaves him. Are there not such persons among those who read this? Perhaps you are among those whom the Lord once used, but He does not use you now. Outwardly you may still be in Christian work, but there is not the old-time liberty and power in it, and this is the reason—you have been untrue to your separation, to your consecration to God. You are listening to Delilah, to the voice of the harlot, to the world and its allurements. Would you get the old power back again? There is but one thing to do. Let your hair grow again as Samson did. Renew your consecration to God.

2. *Power is lost through the incoming of sin.* It was so with Saul, the son of Kish. The Spirit of God came upon Saul and he wrought a great victory for God (I Sam. 11:6ff.). He brought the people of God forward to a place of triumph over their enemies, who had held them under for years. But Saul disobeyed God in two distinct instances (I Sam. 13:13, 14; 15:3, 9-11, 23), and the Lord withdrew His favor and His power; Saul's life ended in utter defeat and ruin. This is the history of many men whom God has once used. Sin has crept in. They have done that which God has told them not to do, or they have refused to do that which God bade them do, and the power of God has been withdrawn.

The one who has known God's power in service, and would continue to know it, must walk very softly before Him. He must be listening constantly to hear what God bids him do or not do. He must respond promptly to the slightest whisper of God. It would seem as if anyone who had once known God's power would rather die than lose it. But it is lost through the incoming of sin. Are there those who are passing through this dreadful experience of the loss of God's power? Ask yourself if this be the reason: Has sin crept in somewhere? Are you doing something, some little thing perhaps, that God tells you not to do? Are you leaving undone something God bids you do? Set this matter right with God and the old power will come back. David was guilty of an awful sin, but when that sin was confessed and put away, he came to know again the power of the Spirit (Ps. 32:1-5; 51:11-13).

If we would continuously know the power of God, we should go often alone with Him, at the close of each day at least, and ask Him to show us if any sin, anything displeasing in His sight, has crept in that day; and if He shows us that there has, we should confess it and put it away then and there.

3. *Power is lost again through self-indulgence.* The one who would have God's power must lead a life of self-denial. There are many things which are not sinful in the ordinary understanding of the word sin, but which hinder spirituality and rob men of power. I do not believe that any man can lead a luxurious life, overindulge his natural appetites, indulge extensively in dainties, and enjoy the fullness of God's power. The gratification of the flesh and the fullness of the Spirit do not go hand

in hand. "The flesh lusteth against the Spirit, and the Spirit against the flesh: and these are contrary the one to the other" (Gal. 5:17). Paul wrote: "I keep under my body, and bring it into subjection" (I Cor. 9:27; see ASV, Greek; note also Eph. 5:18).

We live in a day when the temptation to the indulgence of the flesh is very great. Luxuries are common. Piety and prosperity seldom go hand in hand, and in many a case the prosperity that piety and power have brought has been the ruin of the man to whom it has come. Not a few ministers of power have become popular and in demand. With the increasing popularity has come an increase of pay and of the comforts of life. Luxurious living has come in, and the power of the Spirit has gone out. It would not be difficult to cite specific instances of this sad truth. If we would know the continuance of the Spirit's power, we need to be on guard to lead lives of simplicity, free from indulgence and surfeiting, ever ready to "endure hardness as a good soldier of Jesus Christ" (II Tim. 2:3). I frankly confess I am afraid of luxury—not as afraid of it as I am of sin, but it comes next as an object of dread. It is a very subtle but a very potent enemy of power.

There are devils today that "go not out but by prayer and fasting."

4. *Power is lost through greed for money.* It was through this that a member of the original apostolic company, the twelve whom Jesus himself chose to be with Him, fell. The love of money, the love of accumulation, got into the heart of Judas Iscariot and proved his ruin. "The love of money is a root of all kinds of evil" (I Tim. 6:10, ASV), but one of the greatest evils of which it is the root is that of the loss of spiritual power. How many a man once knew what spiritual power was, but money began to come! He soon felt its strange fascination. The love for accumulation, covetousness, the love for more, little by little, took possession of him. He has accumulated his money honestly; but it has absorbed him, and the Spirit of God is shut out, and his power has departed. Men who would have power need to have the words of Christ: "Take heed and beware of covetousness," written in large letters and engraved deeply upon their hearts. One does not need to be rich to be covetous. A very poor man may be very much absorbed in the desire for wealth—just as much as any greedy millionaire.

5. *Power is lost through pride.* This is the subtlest and most dangerous of all the enemies of power. I am not sure but that more men lose their power at this point than at any other mentioned thus far. There is many a man who has not consciously gone back upon his consecration; he has not let sin, in the sense of conscious doing of that which God forbade or conscious refusal to do that which God commanded, creep into his life; he has not given way to self-indulgence; he has utterly, persistently, and consistently refused the allurements of money accumulation, but still he has failed—*Pride has come in.* He has become puffed up because of the very fact that God has given him power and used him, puffed up it may be over the consistency and simplicity and devotion of his life, and God has been forced to set him aside.

God cannot use a proud man. "God resisteth the proud, and giveth grace to the humble" (I Peter 5:5). The man who is puffed up with pride, self-esteem, cannot be filled up with the Holy Spirit. Paul saw this danger for himself. God saw it for him, and Paul writes. "Lest I should be exalted above measure through the abundance of the revelations, there was given to me a thorn in the flesh, the messenger of Satan to buffet me, lest I should be exalted above measure" (II Cor. 12:7). How many men have failed here! They have sought God's power, sought it in God's way, and it has come. Men have testified of the blessing received through their word, and pride has entered and been indulged, and all is lost.

Moses was the meekest of men, and yet he failed at this very point. "Must we fetch you water out of this rock?" he cried, and then and there God laid him aside (Num. 20:10-12). If God is using us at all, let us get down very low before Him. The more He uses us the lower let us get. May God keep His own words ringing in our ears: "Be clothed with humility: for God resisteth the proud, and giveth grace to the humble" (I Pet. 5:5).

6. *Power is lost through neglect of prayer.* It is in prayer especially that we are charged with the energy of God. It is the man who is much in prayer into whom God's power flows mightily. John Livingston spent a night with some Christians in conference and prayer. The next day (June 21, 1630) he so preached at the

Kirk of Shotts that the Spirit fell upon his hearers in such a way that five hundred could either date their conversion or some remarkable confirmation from that day forward. This is but one instance among thousands to show how power is given in prayer. Virtue or power is constantly going from us, as from Christ (Mark 5:30), in service and blessing; and if power would be maintained, it must be constantly renewed in prayer. When electricity is given off from a charged body it must be recharged. So must we be recharged with the divine energy, and this is effected by coming into contact with God in prayer. Many a man whom God has used becomes lax in his habits of prayer, and the Lord departs from him and his power is gone. Are there not some of us who have not today the power we once had, and simply because we do not spend the time on our faces before God as we once did?

7. *Power is lost through neglect of the Word.* God's power comes through prayer; it comes also through the Word (Ps. 1:2, 3; John 1:8). Many have known the power that comes through the regular, thoughtful, prayerful, protracted meditation upon the Word, but business and perhaps Christian

duties have multiplied, other studies have come in, the Word has been in a measure crowded out, and the power has gone. We must meditate daily, prayerfully, profoundly upon the Word if we are to maintain power. Many a man has run dry through its neglect.

I think the seven points mentioned give the principal ways in which spiritual power is lost. I think of no others. If there is one dread that comes to me more frequently than any other, it is that of losing the power of God. Oh, the agony of having known God's power, of having been used of Him, and then of having that power withdrawn, to be laid aside as far as any real usefulness is concerned! Men may still praise you, but God can't use you.

To see a perishing world around you and to know there is no power in your words to save—would not dying be better than that? I have little fear of losing eternal life. Every believer in Christ has that already. I am in the hand of Jesus Christ and in the hand of God the Father and no one can pluck me out of their hand (John 10:28-30), *but* I see so many men from whom the power of God has departed, men once eminently used of God; I walk with fear and trembling and cry unto Him daily to keep me from the things that would make the withdrawal of His power necessary. But what those things are I think He has made plain to me, and I have tried in the words here written to make them plain to both you and myself.

To sum them up, they are these: the surrender of our separation, sin, self-indulgence, greed for money, pride, the neglect of prayer, and the neglect of the Word. May we by God's grace from this time on be on guard against these things, and thus make sure of the continuance of God's power in our life and service until that glad day comes when we can say with Paul: "I have fought a good fight, I have finished my course, I have kept the faith: henceforth there is laid up for me a crown of righteousness, which the Lord, the righteous judge, shall give me at that day" (II Tim. 4:7, 8). Or better yet, say with Jesus: "I have glorified thee on the earth, having accomplished the work which thou hast given me to do" (John 17:4, ASV).